50 Gluten Free Recipes for Home

By: Kelly Johnson

Table of Contents

- Quinoa and Black Bean Salad
- Almond Flour Pancakes
- Baked Sweet Potato Fries
- Gluten-Free Chicken Parmesan
- Zucchini Noodles with Pesto
- Stuffed Bell Peppers
- Coconut Curry Chicken
- Gluten-Free Meatballs
- Chickpea Flour Frittata
- Roasted Cauliflower Rice
- Greek Salad with Chicken
- Gluten-Free Chocolate Cake
- Spaghetti Squash with Marinara
- Sweet Potato and Kale Hash
- Gluten-Free Beef Tacos
- Almond-Crusted Salmon
- Rice Paper Spring Rolls
- Gluten-Free Banana Bread
- Spicy Shrimp Skewers
- Chicken and Vegetable Stir-Fry
- Gluten-Free Veggie Burgers
- Berry Chia Seed Pudding
- Butternut Squash Soup
- Gluten-Free Quiche
- Cauliflower Pizza Crust
- Apple Cinnamon Oatmeal
- Thai Beef Salad
- Gluten-Free Muffins
- Mediterranean Quinoa Bowl
- Chicken Lettuce Wraps
- Avocado and Tomato Salsa
- Gluten-Free Beef Stew
- Baked Eggplant Parmesan
- Lentil and Vegetable Soup
- Gluten-Free Cornbread

- Honey Garlic Chicken
- Gluten-Free Stuffed Mushrooms
- Cucumber and Hummus Sandwiches
- Baked Lemon Herb Cod
- Chocolate Almond Energy Bites
- Spinach and Feta Stuffed Chicken
- Gluten-Free Pancake Tacos
- Roasted Brussels Sprouts with Bacon
- Sweet and Spicy Pork Tenderloin
- Gluten-Free Pasta Salad
- Savory Butternut Squash Muffins
- Chicken and Avocado Salad
- Gluten-Free Apple Crisp
- Teriyaki Chicken Thighs
- Pumpkin Spice Smoothie

Quinoa and Black Bean Salad

Ingredients:

- 1 cup quinoa
- 1 can (15 oz) black beans, drained and rinsed
- 1 red bell pepper, diced
- 1/2 cup red onion, finely chopped
- 1/2 cup corn kernels (fresh or frozen)
- 1/4 cup fresh cilantro, chopped
- 2 tbsp lime juice
- 3 tbsp olive oil
- Salt and pepper to taste

Instructions:

1. **Cook Quinoa:** Rinse quinoa under cold water. Cook according to package instructions. Let cool.
2. **Combine Ingredients:** In a large bowl, mix cooked quinoa, black beans, bell pepper, red onion, corn, and cilantro.
3. **Make Dressing:** Whisk together lime juice, olive oil, salt, and pepper.
4. **Mix Salad:** Pour dressing over the salad and toss to combine. Serve chilled or at room temperature.

Almond Flour Pancakes

Ingredients:

- 2 cups almond flour
- 1/4 cup coconut flour
- 1/4 tsp salt
- 1/4 tsp baking soda
- 4 large eggs
- 1/4 cup milk (dairy or non-dairy)
- 2 tbsp honey or maple syrup
- 1 tsp vanilla extract
- Coconut oil or butter for cooking

Instructions:

1. **Prepare Batter:** In a bowl, whisk together almond flour, coconut flour, salt, and baking soda. In another bowl, mix eggs, milk, honey, and vanilla. Combine wet and dry ingredients.
2. **Cook Pancakes:** Heat a skillet over medium heat and add a bit of oil or butter. Pour batter onto skillet to form pancakes. Cook until bubbles form on the surface, then flip and cook until golden brown on the other side.
3. **Serve:** Serve warm with your favorite toppings.

Baked Sweet Potato Fries

Ingredients:

- 2 large sweet potatoes, peeled and cut into fries
- 2 tbsp olive oil
- 1/2 tsp paprika
- 1/2 tsp garlic powder
- 1/2 tsp onion powder
- 1/4 tsp salt
- 1/4 tsp black pepper

Instructions:

1. **Prepare Oven:** Preheat oven to 425°F (220°C). Line a baking sheet with parchment paper.
2. **Season Fries:** Toss sweet potato fries with olive oil, paprika, garlic powder, onion powder, salt, and pepper. Spread out on the baking sheet in a single layer.
3. **Bake:** Bake for 20-25 minutes, flipping halfway through, until crispy and golden brown.
4. **Serve:** Serve hot.

Gluten-Free Chicken Parmesan

Ingredients:

- 4 boneless, skinless chicken breasts
- 1 cup gluten-free breadcrumbs
- 1/2 cup grated Parmesan cheese
- 1 cup marinara sauce
- 1 cup shredded mozzarella cheese
- 2 large eggs, beaten
- 1/4 cup all-purpose gluten-free flour
- Olive oil for frying
- Fresh basil for garnish

Instructions:

1. **Prepare Chicken:** Season chicken breasts with salt and pepper. Dredge in gluten-free flour, dip in beaten eggs, and coat with gluten-free breadcrumbs mixed with Parmesan cheese.
2. **Fry Chicken:** Heat olive oil in a skillet over medium heat. Fry chicken until golden and cooked through, about 4-5 minutes per side.
3. **Bake Chicken:** Preheat oven to 375°F (190°C). Place chicken in a baking dish, top with marinara sauce and mozzarella cheese. Bake for 15-20 minutes until cheese is melted and bubbly.
4. **Serve:** Garnish with fresh basil and serve.

Zucchini Noodles with Pesto

Ingredients:

- 4 medium zucchinis, spiralized into noodles
- 1/2 cup pesto sauce
- 1 tbsp olive oil
- Salt and pepper to taste
- Grated Parmesan cheese for garnish (optional)

Instructions:

1. **Cook Zoodles:** Heat olive oil in a skillet over medium heat. Add zucchini noodles and cook for 3-5 minutes, stirring occasionally, until tender but still crisp.
2. **Add Pesto:** Toss zucchini noodles with pesto sauce until well coated.
3. **Serve:** Garnish with grated Parmesan cheese if desired and serve warm.

Stuffed Bell Peppers

Ingredients:

- 4 large bell peppers
- 1 cup cooked rice or quinoa
- 1/2 lb ground beef or turkey
- 1/2 cup onion, finely chopped
- 1 cup marinara sauce
- 1 cup shredded cheese (optional)
- 1 tsp dried oregano
- 1/2 tsp garlic powder
- Salt and pepper to taste

Instructions:

1. **Prepare Peppers:** Preheat oven to 375°F (190°C). Cut tops off bell peppers and remove seeds.
2. **Cook Filling:** In a skillet, cook ground beef or turkey with onions until browned. Stir in rice or quinoa, marinara sauce, oregano, garlic powder, salt, and pepper.
3. **Stuff Peppers:** Fill each bell pepper with the meat mixture. Top with cheese if using. Place peppers in a baking dish.
4. **Bake:** Bake for 25-30 minutes until peppers are tender and filling is hot.
5. **Serve:** Serve warm.

Coconut Curry Chicken

Ingredients:

- 1 lb chicken thighs or breasts, cut into bite-sized pieces
- 1 can (13.5 oz) coconut milk
- 2 tbsp red curry paste
- 1 tbsp fish sauce
- 1 tbsp brown sugar
- 1 red bell pepper, sliced
- 1 cup baby spinach
- 2 tbsp vegetable oil
- Fresh cilantro for garnish

Instructions:

1. **Cook Chicken:** Heat vegetable oil in a pan over medium heat. Add chicken and cook until browned.
2. **Make Curry Sauce:** Stir in red curry paste and cook for 1-2 minutes. Pour in coconut milk, fish sauce, and brown sugar. Bring to a simmer.
3. **Add Vegetables:** Add bell pepper and simmer until chicken is cooked through and vegetables are tender. Stir in spinach until wilted.
4. **Serve:** Garnish with fresh cilantro and serve with rice.

Gluten-Free Meatballs

Ingredients:

- 1 lb ground beef or turkey
- 1/2 cup gluten-free breadcrumbs
- 1/4 cup grated Parmesan cheese
- 1/4 cup chopped parsley
- 1 egg
- 2 cloves garlic, minced
- 1/2 tsp dried oregano
- Salt and pepper to taste
- Olive oil for baking

Instructions:

1. **Prepare Mixture:** In a bowl, mix ground beef or turkey, gluten-free breadcrumbs, Parmesan cheese, parsley, egg, garlic, oregano, salt, and pepper until well combined.
2. **Form Meatballs:** Shape mixture into 1-inch meatballs and place on a baking sheet.
3. **Bake Meatballs:** Drizzle with olive oil and bake at 375°F (190°C) for 20-25 minutes, until cooked through.
4. **Serve:** Serve with marinara sauce or your favorite dipping sauce.

Chickpea Flour Frittata

Ingredients:

- 1 cup chickpea flour
- 1 1/4 cups water
- 1 tbsp olive oil
- 1 cup spinach, chopped
- 1/2 cup cherry tomatoes, halved
- 1/4 cup red onion, finely chopped
- 1/4 cup nutritional yeast
- 1/2 tsp turmeric
- 1/4 tsp garlic powder
- Salt and pepper to taste

Instructions:

1. **Prepare Batter:** In a bowl, whisk chickpea flour with water until smooth. Stir in nutritional yeast, turmeric, garlic powder, salt, and pepper.
2. **Cook Vegetables:** Heat olive oil in a skillet over medium heat. Sauté red onion until softened, then add spinach and tomatoes. Cook for a few minutes until spinach is wilted.
3. **Combine and Cook:** Pour the chickpea flour mixture over the vegetables. Cook over medium heat until the edges start to set, then transfer to a preheated oven (375°F/190°C) and bake for 15-20 minutes, or until firm and golden brown.
4. **Serve:** Let cool slightly before slicing. Serve warm or at room temperature.

Roasted Cauliflower Rice

Ingredients:

- 1 head cauliflower, cut into florets
- 2 tbsp olive oil
- 1/2 tsp garlic powder
- 1/2 tsp onion powder
- Salt and pepper to taste

Instructions:

1. **Prepare Cauliflower:** Preheat oven to 425°F (220°C). In a food processor, pulse cauliflower florets until they resemble rice grains.
2. **Season and Roast:** Toss cauliflower rice with olive oil, garlic powder, onion powder, salt, and pepper. Spread out on a baking sheet in a single layer.
3. **Roast:** Roast for 20-25 minutes, stirring halfway through, until cauliflower is tender and slightly golden.
4. **Serve:** Fluff with a fork and serve as a side or base for various dishes.

Greek Salad with Chicken

Ingredients:

- 2 cups cooked chicken breast, sliced
- 2 cups mixed greens
- 1 cup cherry tomatoes, halved
- 1/2 cucumber, sliced
- 1/4 cup red onion, thinly sliced
- 1/4 cup Kalamata olives
- 1/4 cup feta cheese, crumbled
- 2 tbsp olive oil
- 1 tbsp red wine vinegar
- 1/2 tsp dried oregano
- Salt and pepper to taste

Instructions:

1. **Prepare Salad:** In a large bowl, combine mixed greens, cherry tomatoes, cucumber, red onion, olives, and feta cheese.
2. **Make Dressing:** Whisk together olive oil, red wine vinegar, oregano, salt, and pepper.
3. **Combine:** Toss salad with dressing. Top with sliced chicken and serve.

Gluten-Free Chocolate Cake

Ingredients:

- 1 1/2 cups gluten-free all-purpose flour
- 1 cup granulated sugar
- 1/2 cup unsweetened cocoa powder
- 1 tsp baking powder
- 1/2 tsp baking soda
- 1/4 tsp salt
- 2 large eggs
- 1/2 cup vegetable oil
- 1 cup buttermilk
- 1 tsp vanilla extract
- 1 cup boiling water

Instructions:

1. **Prepare Oven and Pans:** Preheat oven to 350°F (175°C). Grease and flour two 8-inch round cake pans.
2. **Mix Dry Ingredients:** In a bowl, sift together flour, sugar, cocoa powder, baking powder, baking soda, and salt.
3. **Mix Wet Ingredients:** In another bowl, beat eggs, oil, buttermilk, and vanilla. Add to dry ingredients and mix until combined. Stir in boiling water until smooth.
4. **Bake:** Divide batter evenly between pans. Bake for 30-35 minutes, or until a toothpick inserted in the center comes out clean. Cool in pans for 10 minutes, then transfer to wire racks to cool completely.
5. **Frost:** Frost with your favorite gluten-free frosting and serve.

Spaghetti Squash with Marinara

Ingredients:

- 1 medium spaghetti squash
- 2 cups marinara sauce
- 2 tbsp olive oil
- 1/2 tsp garlic powder
- 1/2 tsp dried basil
- Salt and pepper to taste
- Grated Parmesan cheese for serving (optional)

Instructions:

1. **Prepare Squash:** Preheat oven to 400°F (200°C). Cut spaghetti squash in half lengthwise and scoop out seeds. Drizzle with olive oil, garlic powder, basil, salt, and pepper.
2. **Roast:** Place cut-side down on a baking sheet and roast for 40-45 minutes until tender.
3. **Scrape and Serve:** Use a fork to scrape out the spaghetti-like strands. Top with warm marinara sauce and garnish with Parmesan cheese if desired.

Sweet Potato and Kale Hash

Ingredients:

- 2 large sweet potatoes, peeled and diced
- 1 tbsp olive oil
- 1 onion, diced
- 2 cloves garlic, minced
- 2 cups kale, chopped
- 1/2 tsp smoked paprika
- 1/4 tsp cumin
- Salt and pepper to taste

Instructions:

1. **Cook Sweet Potatoes:** Heat olive oil in a skillet over medium heat. Add sweet potatoes and cook, stirring occasionally, until tender and lightly browned, about 10-15 minutes.
2. **Add Vegetables:** Stir in onion and garlic and cook until onion is translucent.
3. **Add Kale:** Add kale and cook until wilted. Season with smoked paprika, cumin, salt, and pepper.
4. **Serve:** Serve warm.

Gluten-Free Beef Tacos

Ingredients:

- 1 lb ground beef
- 1 tbsp taco seasoning (gluten-free)
- 1/4 cup water
- 8 gluten-free taco shells
- 1 cup shredded lettuce
- 1/2 cup diced tomatoes
- 1/2 cup shredded cheese
- 1/4 cup sour cream
- Salsa or guacamole (optional)

Instructions:

1. **Cook Beef:** In a skillet, cook ground beef over medium heat until browned. Drain excess fat.
2. **Season Beef:** Stir in taco seasoning and water. Simmer for 5 minutes until the sauce thickens.
3. **Assemble Tacos:** Fill taco shells with seasoned beef, lettuce, tomatoes, and cheese. Top with sour cream and salsa or guacamole if desired.
4. **Serve:** Serve immediately.

Almond-Crusted Salmon

Ingredients:

- 4 salmon fillets
- 1/2 cup almond flour
- 1/4 cup grated Parmesan cheese
- 1/2 tsp dried thyme
- 1/2 tsp dried rosemary
- 1/4 tsp garlic powder
- 1 egg, beaten
- Salt and pepper to taste
- Olive oil for baking

Instructions:

1. **Prepare Oven and Baking Sheet:** Preheat oven to 400°F (200°C). Line a baking sheet with parchment paper.
2. **Prepare Coating:** In a bowl, mix almond flour, Parmesan cheese, thyme, rosemary, garlic powder, salt, and pepper.
3. **Coat Salmon:** Dip each salmon fillet in beaten egg, then coat with almond mixture. Place on the baking sheet.
4. **Bake:** Bake for 12-15 minutes, or until salmon is cooked through and the coating is golden brown.
5. **Serve:** Serve warm with your choice of sides.

Rice Paper Spring Rolls

Ingredients:

- 12 rice paper wrappers
- 1 cup cooked rice noodles
- 1 cup shredded lettuce
- 1 cup julienned carrots
- 1/2 cup cucumber, julienned
- 1/2 cup fresh mint leaves
- 1/2 cup fresh basil leaves
- 1/2 cup cooked shrimp, sliced (optional)
- 1/4 cup hoisin sauce (for dipping)

Instructions:

1. **Prepare Filling:** Arrange cooked rice noodles, lettuce, carrots, cucumber, mint, basil, and shrimp (if using) in a bowl.
2. **Soften Rice Paper:** Fill a large bowl with warm water. Dip one rice paper wrapper into the water for about 10-15 seconds, or until soft and pliable.
3. **Assemble Rolls:** Lay the softened rice paper on a clean surface. Place a small amount of the filling ingredients in the center. Fold the sides over the filling, then roll from the bottom up, tucking in the sides as you go.
4. **Serve:** Repeat with remaining wrappers and filling. Serve with hoisin sauce for dipping.

Gluten-Free Banana Bread

Ingredients:

- 3 ripe bananas, mashed
- 1/2 cup coconut oil, melted
- 1/2 cup honey or maple syrup
- 2 large eggs
- 1 tsp vanilla extract
- 1 1/2 cups gluten-free all-purpose flour
- 1 tsp baking soda
- 1/4 tsp salt
- 1/2 cup chopped walnuts or chocolate chips (optional)

Instructions:

1. **Prepare Oven and Pan:** Preheat oven to 350°F (175°C). Grease and flour a loaf pan.
2. **Mix Wet Ingredients:** In a bowl, mix mashed bananas, melted coconut oil, honey or maple syrup, eggs, and vanilla extract until well combined.
3. **Add Dry Ingredients:** In another bowl, whisk together gluten-free flour, baking soda, and salt. Gradually add to the banana mixture, stirring until just combined. Fold in walnuts or chocolate chips if using.
4. **Bake:** Pour batter into the prepared loaf pan. Bake for 55-60 minutes, or until a toothpick inserted into the center comes out clean. Let cool before slicing.

Spicy Shrimp Skewers

Ingredients:

- 1 lb large shrimp, peeled and deveined
- 2 tbsp olive oil
- 2 tbsp sriracha sauce
- 1 tbsp honey
- 1 tsp smoked paprika
- 1/2 tsp garlic powder
- 1/2 tsp onion powder
- Salt and pepper to taste
- Lemon wedges for serving

Instructions:

1. **Prepare Marinade:** In a bowl, whisk together olive oil, sriracha, honey, smoked paprika, garlic powder, onion powder, salt, and pepper.
2. **Marinate Shrimp:** Toss shrimp in the marinade and let sit for 15-20 minutes.
3. **Preheat Grill:** Preheat grill to medium-high heat. Thread shrimp onto skewers.
4. **Grill:** Grill shrimp for 2-3 minutes per side, or until pink and cooked through.
5. **Serve:** Serve with lemon wedges.

Chicken and Vegetable Stir-Fry

Ingredients:

- 1 lb chicken breast, thinly sliced
- 2 tbsp olive oil
- 1 cup broccoli florets
- 1 red bell pepper, sliced
- 1 cup snap peas
- 1 carrot, julienned
- 1/4 cup soy sauce (gluten-free if needed)
- 2 tbsp hoisin sauce
- 1 tbsp cornstarch mixed with 2 tbsp water (for thickening)
- Cooked rice for serving

Instructions:

1. **Cook Chicken:** Heat olive oil in a large skillet or wok over medium-high heat. Add chicken and cook until no longer pink, about 5-6 minutes. Remove from skillet and set aside.
2. **Stir-Fry Vegetables:** In the same skillet, add broccoli, bell pepper, snap peas, and carrot. Stir-fry for 4-5 minutes until tender-crisp.
3. **Combine and Sauce:** Return chicken to the skillet. Add soy sauce and hoisin sauce. Stir in cornstarch mixture and cook until the sauce has thickened, about 2 minutes.
4. **Serve:** Serve over cooked rice.

Gluten-Free Veggie Burgers

Ingredients:

- 1 can (15 oz) black beans, drained and rinsed
- 1/2 cup grated carrot
- 1/2 cup finely chopped onion
- 1/2 cup gluten-free breadcrumbs
- 1/4 cup chopped fresh parsley
- 1 egg, beaten
- 1 tbsp olive oil
- 1/2 tsp cumin
- 1/2 tsp paprika
- Salt and pepper to taste

Instructions:

1. **Prepare Mixture:** In a bowl, mash black beans until mostly smooth. Stir in grated carrot, onion, gluten-free breadcrumbs, parsley, egg, olive oil, cumin, paprika, salt, and pepper. Mix until combined.
2. **Form Patties:** Shape mixture into 4-6 patties.
3. **Cook Patties:** Heat olive oil in a skillet over medium heat. Cook patties for 4-5 minutes per side, or until golden brown and crispy.
4. **Serve:** Serve on gluten-free buns with desired toppings.

Berry Chia Seed Pudding

Ingredients:

- 1/4 cup chia seeds
- 1 cup almond milk (or any milk of choice)
- 1 tbsp maple syrup or honey
- 1/2 tsp vanilla extract
- 1/2 cup mixed berries (fresh or frozen)

Instructions:

1. **Mix Pudding:** In a bowl, combine chia seeds, almond milk, maple syrup, and vanilla extract. Stir well.
2. **Refrigerate:** Cover and refrigerate for at least 4 hours, or overnight, until it thickens.
3. **Serve:** Stir pudding before serving and top with mixed berries.

Butternut Squash Soup

Ingredients:

- 1 large butternut squash, peeled, seeded, and cubed
- 1 tbsp olive oil
- 1 onion, chopped
- 2 cloves garlic, minced
- 4 cups vegetable or chicken broth
- 1/2 tsp ground cumin
- 1/2 tsp ground cinnamon
- Salt and pepper to taste
- 1/2 cup coconut milk (optional)

Instructions:

1. **Roast Squash:** Preheat oven to 400°F (200°C). Toss butternut squash with olive oil, salt, and pepper. Spread on a baking sheet and roast for 25-30 minutes, until tender.
2. **Cook Aromatics:** In a large pot, heat olive oil over medium heat. Add onion and garlic, and cook until softened.
3. **Combine and Simmer:** Add roasted squash, broth, cumin, and cinnamon to the pot. Bring to a boil, then reduce heat and simmer for 10 minutes.
4. **Blend and Serve:** Use an immersion blender to blend soup until smooth. Stir in coconut milk if using. Serve warm.

Gluten-Free Quiche

Ingredients:

- 1 gluten-free pie crust
- 6 large eggs
- 1 cup heavy cream
- 1 cup shredded cheese (cheddar, Swiss, or your choice)
- 1/2 cup cooked bacon or ham, chopped
- 1/2 cup chopped spinach
- 1/4 cup chopped onion
- Salt and pepper to taste

Instructions:

1. **Preheat Oven:** Preheat oven to 375°F (190°C).
2. **Prepare Crust:** Place the gluten-free pie crust in a pie dish.
3. **Mix Filling:** In a bowl, whisk together eggs and heavy cream. Stir in cheese, bacon or ham, spinach, onion, salt, and pepper.
4. **Pour and Bake:** Pour the mixture into the pie crust. Bake for 35-40 minutes, or until the quiche is set and the top is golden brown. Let cool slightly before slicing.

Cauliflower Pizza Crust

Ingredients:

- 1 large head of cauliflower, cut into florets
- 1 cup shredded mozzarella cheese
- 1/4 cup grated Parmesan cheese
- 1 large egg
- 1/2 tsp dried oregano
- 1/2 tsp dried basil
- 1/2 tsp garlic powder
- Salt and pepper to taste

Instructions:

1. **Preheat Oven:** Preheat oven to 425°F (220°C). Line a baking sheet with parchment paper.
2. **Prepare Cauliflower:** In a food processor, pulse cauliflower florets until they resemble rice or crumbs. Transfer to a microwave-safe bowl and microwave for 5-6 minutes, or until tender. Let cool slightly.
3. **Drain and Mix:** Place the cauliflower in a clean kitchen towel and squeeze out as much moisture as possible. In a bowl, combine cauliflower, mozzarella cheese, Parmesan cheese, egg, oregano, basil, garlic powder, salt, and pepper.
4. **Form Crust:** Spread the mixture onto the prepared baking sheet, forming a pizza crust shape. Bake for 15-20 minutes, or until the crust is golden brown.
5. **Add Toppings:** Add desired pizza toppings and bake for an additional 5-10 minutes.

Apple Cinnamon Oatmeal

Ingredients:

- 1 cup rolled oats
- 1 1/2 cups milk (or dairy-free alternative)
- 1 apple, peeled and diced
- 1/4 cup maple syrup or honey
- 1/2 tsp ground cinnamon
- 1/4 tsp vanilla extract
- A pinch of salt

Instructions:

1. **Cook Oats:** In a medium saucepan, bring milk to a boil. Stir in oats, reduce heat, and simmer for 5 minutes.
2. **Add Apples and Flavorings:** Stir in diced apple, maple syrup or honey, cinnamon, vanilla extract, and salt. Continue cooking for an additional 5 minutes, or until the oats are tender and the apples are soft.
3. **Serve:** Serve warm, topped with extra apples, nuts, or a drizzle of maple syrup if desired.

Thai Beef Salad

Ingredients:

- 1 lb beef sirloin, thinly sliced
- 4 cups mixed salad greens
- 1 cup cherry tomatoes, halved
- 1/2 cup cucumber, sliced
- 1/4 cup red onion, thinly sliced
- 1/4 cup fresh cilantro, chopped
- 1/4 cup fresh mint leaves
- 2 tbsp fish sauce
- 1 tbsp lime juice
- 1 tbsp brown sugar
- 1-2 red chili peppers, sliced (optional)

Instructions:

1. **Cook Beef:** Heat a grill or skillet over high heat. Cook beef slices for 2-3 minutes per side, or until cooked to your liking. Remove from heat and let rest.
2. **Prepare Dressing:** In a bowl, whisk together fish sauce, lime juice, brown sugar, and red chili peppers (if using).
3. **Assemble Salad:** In a large bowl, combine salad greens, cherry tomatoes, cucumber, red onion, cilantro, and mint. Slice the beef and add to the salad.
4. **Dress and Serve:** Drizzle with dressing and toss to combine. Serve immediately.

Gluten-Free Muffins

Ingredients:

- 1 1/2 cups gluten-free all-purpose flour
- 1/2 cup sugar
- 1/2 cup milk (or dairy-free alternative)
- 1/4 cup vegetable oil
- 2 large eggs
- 1 tsp baking powder
- 1/2 tsp baking soda
- 1/4 tsp salt
- 1/2 cup blueberries or chocolate chips (optional)

Instructions:

1. **Preheat Oven:** Preheat oven to 350°F (175°C). Line a muffin tin with paper liners or grease.
2. **Mix Dry Ingredients:** In a bowl, whisk together gluten-free flour, sugar, baking powder, baking soda, and salt.
3. **Mix Wet Ingredients:** In another bowl, whisk together milk, vegetable oil, and eggs.
4. **Combine and Fold:** Add wet ingredients to dry ingredients and mix until just combined. Fold in blueberries or chocolate chips if using.
5. **Bake:** Divide batter among muffin cups. Bake for 18-20 minutes, or until a toothpick inserted into the center comes out clean. Let cool before serving.

Mediterranean Quinoa Bowl

Ingredients:

- 1 cup quinoa, rinsed
- 2 cups water or vegetable broth
- 1 cup cherry tomatoes, halved
- 1 cucumber, diced
- 1/2 cup Kalamata olives, sliced
- 1/4 cup red onion, thinly sliced
- 1/4 cup crumbled feta cheese
- 2 tbsp olive oil
- 2 tbsp lemon juice
- 1 tsp dried oregano
- Salt and pepper to taste

Instructions:

1. **Cook Quinoa:** In a saucepan, bring water or broth to a boil. Add quinoa, reduce heat, and simmer for 15 minutes, or until quinoa is tender and liquid is absorbed. Let cool.
2. **Prepare Salad:** In a large bowl, combine cooked quinoa, cherry tomatoes, cucumber, olives, red onion, and feta cheese.
3. **Dress and Serve:** In a small bowl, whisk together olive oil, lemon juice, oregano, salt, and pepper. Drizzle over the salad and toss to combine. Serve chilled or at room temperature.

Chicken Lettuce Wraps

Ingredients:

- 1 lb ground chicken
- 1 tbsp olive oil
- 1/2 cup diced onion
- 2 cloves garlic, minced
- 1/2 cup diced bell pepper
- 1/4 cup soy sauce (gluten-free if needed)
- 1 tbsp hoisin sauce
- 1 tbsp rice vinegar
- 1/2 tsp grated ginger
- 1/4 cup chopped fresh cilantro
- Lettuce leaves for wrapping

Instructions:

1. **Cook Chicken:** Heat olive oil in a skillet over medium heat. Add ground chicken and cook until browned. Remove excess fat if necessary.
2. **Add Vegetables and Sauce:** Add onion, garlic, and bell pepper to the skillet. Cook until vegetables are tender. Stir in soy sauce, hoisin sauce, rice vinegar, and ginger.
3. **Finish and Serve:** Cook for an additional 2-3 minutes, until sauce is thickened. Stir in cilantro. Spoon the mixture into lettuce leaves and serve.

Avocado and Tomato Salsa

Ingredients:

- 2 ripe avocados, diced
- 1 cup cherry tomatoes, halved
- 1/4 cup red onion, finely chopped
- 2 tbsp fresh cilantro, chopped
- 1 tbsp lime juice
- Salt and pepper to taste

Instructions:

1. **Combine Ingredients:** In a bowl, gently mix together avocados, cherry tomatoes, red onion, and cilantro.
2. **Season:** Drizzle with lime juice and season with salt and pepper.
3. **Serve:** Serve immediately with tortilla chips or as a topping for grilled meats.

Gluten-Free Beef Stew

Ingredients:

- 2 lbs beef stew meat, cut into cubes
- 1 tbsp olive oil
- 1 onion, diced
- 3 cloves garlic, minced
- 4 cups beef broth (gluten-free)
- 4 carrots, sliced
- 3 potatoes, diced
- 1 cup celery, sliced
- 1 cup frozen peas
- 1 tbsp tomato paste
- 1 tsp dried thyme
- 1 tsp dried rosemary
- Salt and pepper to taste
- 2 tbsp gluten-free flour or cornstarch (optional, for thickening)

Instructions:

1. **Brown Beef:** Heat olive oil in a large pot over medium-high heat. Add beef cubes and brown on all sides. Remove beef and set aside.
2. **Cook Vegetables:** In the same pot, add onion and garlic, and cook until softened. Stir in tomato paste and cook for 1 minute.
3. **Simmer Stew:** Return beef to the pot. Add beef broth, carrots, potatoes, celery, thyme, and rosemary. Bring to a boil, then reduce heat and simmer for 1-2 hours, or until beef is tender.
4. **Thicken (Optional):** If desired, mix gluten-free flour or cornstarch with a small amount of water to form a slurry, then stir into the stew and cook for an additional 5-10 minutes to thicken. Stir in peas just before serving.

Baked Eggplant Parmesan

Ingredients:

- 1 large eggplant, sliced into 1/4-inch rounds
- 1 cup gluten-free breadcrumbs
- 1/2 cup grated Parmesan cheese
- 2 cups marinara sauce
- 2 cups shredded mozzarella cheese
- 2 large eggs, beaten
- 1/2 cup all-purpose gluten-free flour
- 1/4 cup olive oil
- 1 tsp dried oregano
- 1 tsp dried basil
- Salt and pepper to taste

Instructions:

1. **Preheat Oven:** Preheat oven to 375°F (190°C).
2. **Prepare Eggplant:** Sprinkle eggplant slices with salt and let sit for 20 minutes to draw out moisture. Rinse and pat dry.
3. **Bread and Bake:** Set up a breading station with flour, beaten eggs, and a mixture of gluten-free breadcrumbs, Parmesan cheese, oregano, basil, salt, and pepper. Dip eggplant slices in flour, then egg, then breadcrumb mixture. Arrange on a baking sheet and brush with olive oil. Bake for 20-25 minutes, or until golden brown.
4. **Assemble and Bake:** Spread a thin layer of marinara sauce in a baking dish. Layer baked eggplant slices with marinara sauce and mozzarella cheese. Repeat layers and top with remaining cheese. Bake for 20-25 minutes, or until bubbly and golden.

Lentil and Vegetable Soup

Ingredients:

- 1 cup dried lentils, rinsed
- 1 tbsp olive oil
- 1 onion, diced
- 2 cloves garlic, minced
- 2 carrots, diced
- 2 celery stalks, diced
- 1 bell pepper, diced
- 1 cup diced tomatoes
- 4 cups vegetable broth
- 1 tsp dried thyme
- 1 tsp dried basil
- 1 bay leaf
- Salt and pepper to taste
- 2 cups spinach or kale (optional)

Instructions:

1. **Cook Vegetables:** Heat olive oil in a large pot over medium heat. Add onion and garlic, and cook until softened. Add carrots, celery, and bell pepper, and cook for another 5 minutes.
2. **Simmer Soup:** Stir in lentils, tomatoes, vegetable broth, thyme, basil, and bay leaf. Bring to a boil, then reduce heat and simmer for 30-40 minutes, or until lentils are tender.
3. **Finish and Serve:** Season with salt and pepper. Stir in spinach or kale if using, and cook until wilted. Serve warm.

Gluten-Free Cornbread

Ingredients:

- 1 cup cornmeal
- 1 cup gluten-free all-purpose flour
- 1/4 cup sugar
- 1 tbsp baking powder
- 1/2 tsp salt
- 1 cup milk (or dairy-free alternative)
- 2 large eggs
- 1/4 cup vegetable oil or melted butter

Instructions:

1. **Preheat Oven:** Preheat oven to 400°F (200°C). Grease a baking dish or line with parchment paper.
2. **Mix Dry Ingredients:** In a bowl, whisk together cornmeal, gluten-free flour, sugar, baking powder, and salt.
3. **Mix Wet Ingredients:** In another bowl, whisk together milk, eggs, and vegetable oil or melted butter.
4. **Combine and Bake:** Add wet ingredients to dry ingredients and mix until just combined. Pour batter into the prepared dish and bake for 20-25 minutes, or until golden brown and a toothpick inserted into the center comes out clean.

Honey Garlic Chicken

Ingredients:

- 1 lb chicken thighs or breasts, cut into bite-sized pieces
- 2 tbsp olive oil
- 1/4 cup honey
- 1/4 cup soy sauce (gluten-free if needed)
- 3 cloves garlic, minced
- 1 tbsp rice vinegar
- 1 tbsp cornstarch (optional, for thickening)
- 1 tbsp water (for cornstarch slurry)
- Sesame seeds and chopped green onions for garnish (optional)

Instructions:

1. **Cook Chicken:** Heat olive oil in a skillet over medium heat. Add chicken pieces and cook until browned and cooked through. Remove chicken and set aside.
2. **Prepare Sauce:** In the same skillet, combine honey, soy sauce, garlic, and rice vinegar. Bring to a simmer.
3. **Thicken Sauce (Optional):** If desired, mix cornstarch with water to create a slurry, then stir into the sauce and cook until thickened.
4. **Combine and Serve:** Return chicken to the skillet and toss to coat with the sauce. Cook for an additional 2-3 minutes. Garnish with sesame seeds and green onions if desired.

Gluten-Free Stuffed Mushrooms

Ingredients:

- 12 large mushroom caps
- 1/2 cup gluten-free breadcrumbs
- 1/4 cup grated Parmesan cheese
- 1/4 cup cream cheese, softened
- 2 cloves garlic, minced
- 1/4 cup chopped fresh parsley
- 1 tbsp olive oil
- Salt and pepper to taste

Instructions:

1. **Preheat Oven:** Preheat oven to 375°F (190°C).
2. **Prepare Filling:** In a bowl, mix together gluten-free breadcrumbs, Parmesan cheese, cream cheese, garlic, parsley, olive oil, salt, and pepper.
3. **Stuff Mushrooms:** Remove stems from mushroom caps and fill each cap with the stuffing mixture. Arrange stuffed mushrooms on a baking sheet.
4. **Bake:** Bake for 15-20 minutes, or until mushrooms are tender and filling is golden. Serve warm.

Cucumber and Hummus Sandwiches

Ingredients:

- 1 cucumber, thinly sliced
- 1/2 cup hummus (store-bought or homemade)
- 8 slices gluten-free bread
- Fresh dill or parsley for garnish (optional)

Instructions:

1. **Prepare Bread:** Spread hummus evenly on one side of each slice of bread.
2. **Assemble Sandwiches:** Layer cucumber slices on half of the bread slices, then top with remaining bread slices.
3. **Cut and Garnish:** Cut sandwiches into triangles or quarters. Garnish with fresh dill or parsley if desired. Serve immediately.

Baked Lemon Herb Cod

Ingredients:

- 4 cod fillets
- 2 tbsp olive oil
- Juice of 1 lemon
- 1 tsp dried thyme
- 1 tsp dried basil
- 1/2 tsp garlic powder
- Salt and pepper to taste
- Lemon wedges for serving

Instructions:

1. **Preheat Oven:** Preheat oven to 400°F (200°C).
2. **Prepare Cod:** Place cod fillets on a baking sheet lined with parchment paper. Drizzle with olive oil and lemon juice.
3. **Season:** Sprinkle with thyme, basil, garlic powder, salt, and pepper.
4. **Bake:** Bake for 15-20 minutes, or until fish flakes easily with a fork. Serve with lemon wedges.

Chocolate Almond Energy Bites

Ingredients:

- 1 cup almonds
- 1 cup pitted dates
- 1/2 cup unsweetened cocoa powder
- 1/4 cup honey or maple syrup
- 1/4 cup almond butter
- 1/4 cup mini chocolate chips (optional)
- 1/2 tsp vanilla extract

Instructions:

1. **Process Nuts and Dates:** In a food processor, pulse almonds until finely chopped. Add dates and process until mixture starts to clump together.
2. **Combine Ingredients:** Add cocoa powder, honey or maple syrup, almond butter, and vanilla extract. Process until well combined. Stir in chocolate chips if using.
3. **Form Bites:** Roll mixture into 1-inch balls and place on a parchment-lined baking sheet.
4. **Chill:** Refrigerate for at least 30 minutes before serving. Store in an airtight container in the fridge for up to 2 weeks.

Spinach and Feta Stuffed Chicken

Ingredients:

- 4 boneless, skinless chicken breasts
- 1 cup fresh spinach, chopped
- 1/2 cup crumbled feta cheese
- 2 cloves garlic, minced
- 1 tbsp olive oil
- 1 tsp dried oregano
- Salt and pepper to taste

Instructions:

1. **Prepare Filling:** In a bowl, mix together spinach, feta cheese, and garlic.
2. **Stuff Chicken:** Cut a pocket into each chicken breast. Stuff with spinach and feta mixture. Secure with toothpicks if necessary.
3. **Season and Cook:** Rub chicken with olive oil, oregano, salt, and pepper. Heat a skillet over medium-high heat. Cook chicken for 5-6 minutes per side, or until cooked through.
4. **Serve:** Let rest for a few minutes before slicing. Serve warm.

Gluten-Free Pancake Tacos

Ingredients:

- 1 cup gluten-free pancake mix
- 1 cup milk (dairy or non-dairy)
- 1 egg
- 2 tbsp melted butter or oil
- Filling of choice (e.g., scrambled eggs, bacon, avocado, cheese)

Instructions:

1. **Prepare Pancake Batter:** In a bowl, mix pancake mix, milk, egg, and melted butter or oil until smooth.
2. **Cook Pancakes:** Heat a non-stick skillet over medium heat. Pour batter to form small pancakes (about 4 inches in diameter). Cook until bubbles form, then flip and cook until golden brown.
3. **Assemble Tacos:** Fill pancakes with desired toppings to create taco-like wraps. Serve warm.

Roasted Brussels Sprouts with Bacon

Ingredients:

- 1 lb Brussels sprouts, trimmed and halved
- 4 slices bacon, diced
- 2 tbsp olive oil
- Salt and pepper to taste

Instructions:

1. **Preheat Oven:** Preheat oven to 400°F (200°C).
2. **Prepare Vegetables:** Toss Brussels sprouts with olive oil, salt, and pepper. Spread out on a baking sheet.
3. **Add Bacon:** Sprinkle diced bacon over the Brussels sprouts.
4. **Roast:** Roast for 20-25 minutes, stirring halfway through, until Brussels sprouts are tender and bacon is crispy.

Sweet and Spicy Pork Tenderloin

Ingredients:

- 1 lb pork tenderloin
- 2 tbsp honey
- 2 tbsp soy sauce (gluten-free if needed)
- 1 tbsp Sriracha sauce
- 2 cloves garlic, minced
- 1 tbsp olive oil
- Salt and pepper to taste

Instructions:

1. **Prepare Marinade:** In a bowl, mix honey, soy sauce, Sriracha sauce, and garlic.
2. **Marinate Pork:** Season pork tenderloin with salt and pepper. Coat with marinade and let sit for at least 30 minutes.
3. **Cook Pork:** Heat olive oil in a skillet over medium-high heat. Cook pork for 4-5 minutes per side, or until cooked through and caramelized. Let rest for 5 minutes before slicing.

Gluten-Free Pasta Salad

Ingredients:

- 8 oz gluten-free pasta
- 1 cup cherry tomatoes, halved
- 1/2 cup black olives, sliced
- 1/2 cup diced cucumber
- 1/4 cup chopped red onion
- 1/4 cup feta cheese (optional)
- 1/4 cup olive oil
- 2 tbsp red wine vinegar
- 1 tsp dried oregano
- Salt and pepper to taste

Instructions:

1. **Cook Pasta:** Cook gluten-free pasta according to package instructions. Drain and let cool.
2. **Prepare Salad:** In a large bowl, combine pasta, cherry tomatoes, olives, cucumber, red onion, and feta cheese.
3. **Make Dressing:** Whisk together olive oil, red wine vinegar, oregano, salt, and pepper.
4. **Toss Salad:** Pour dressing over salad and toss to combine. Serve chilled or at room temperature.

Savory Butternut Squash Muffins

Ingredients:

- 1 cup butternut squash puree
- 2 cups gluten-free all-purpose flour
- 1/2 cup grated Parmesan cheese
- 1/2 cup chopped fresh sage
- 1/4 cup olive oil
- 1/4 cup honey
- 2 large eggs
- 1 tbsp baking powder
- 1/2 tsp salt

Instructions:

1. **Preheat Oven:** Preheat oven to 375°F (190°C). Grease or line a muffin tin.
2. **Mix Ingredients:** In a large bowl, mix together flour, Parmesan cheese, sage, baking powder, and salt. In another bowl, whisk together butternut squash puree, olive oil, honey, and eggs.
3. **Combine:** Add wet ingredients to dry ingredients and stir until just combined.
4. **Bake:** Divide batter among muffin cups. Bake for 18-20 minutes, or until a toothpick inserted into the center comes out clean. Let cool before serving.

Chicken and Avocado Salad

Ingredients:

- 2 cups cooked chicken, diced
- 1 avocado, diced
- 1/2 cup cherry tomatoes, halved
- 1/4 cup red onion, finely chopped
- 1/4 cup chopped fresh cilantro
- Juice of 1 lime
- 2 tbsp olive oil
- Salt and pepper to taste

Instructions:

1. **Combine Ingredients:** In a large bowl, mix together chicken, avocado, cherry tomatoes, red onion, and cilantro.
2. **Dress Salad:** Drizzle with lime juice and olive oil. Season with salt and pepper.
3. **Serve:** Toss to combine and serve immediately or chill before serving.

Gluten-Free Apple Crisp

Ingredients:

- **For the Filling:**
    - 6 cups apples, peeled, cored, and sliced
    - 1/2 cup granulated sugar
    - 1 tbsp lemon juice
    - 1 tsp ground cinnamon
    - 1/4 tsp ground nutmeg
- **For the Topping:**
    - 1 cup gluten-free rolled oats
    - 1/2 cup almond flour
    - 1/2 cup brown sugar
    - 1/4 cup coconut oil, melted
    - 1/2 tsp ground cinnamon
    - Pinch of salt

Instructions:

1. **Prepare Filling:** Preheat oven to 350°F (175°C). In a large bowl, combine sliced apples, sugar, lemon juice, cinnamon, and nutmeg. Mix well and transfer to a greased 9x13-inch baking dish.
2. **Prepare Topping:** In a separate bowl, mix oats, almond flour, brown sugar, melted coconut oil, cinnamon, and salt.
3. **Assemble and Bake:** Sprinkle topping evenly over the apple mixture. Bake for 40-45 minutes, or until the topping is golden brown and the filling is bubbling. Let cool slightly before serving.

Teriyaki Chicken Thighs

Ingredients:

- 6 boneless, skinless chicken thighs
- 1/2 cup low-sodium soy sauce (gluten-free if needed)
- 1/4 cup honey
- 1/4 cup rice vinegar
- 2 cloves garlic, minced
- 1 tbsp freshly grated ginger
- 1 tbsp cornstarch (optional, for thickening)
- 2 tbsp water (if using cornstarch)

Instructions:

1. **Prepare Marinade:** In a bowl, whisk together soy sauce, honey, rice vinegar, garlic, and ginger.
2. **Marinate Chicken:** Place chicken thighs in a resealable bag or dish and pour marinade over them. Seal and refrigerate for at least 1 hour or overnight.
3. **Cook Chicken:** Preheat grill or skillet over medium heat. Cook chicken for 5-7 minutes per side, or until fully cooked and internal temperature reaches 165°F (74°C).
4. **Thicken Sauce (Optional):** If desired, mix cornstarch with water and add to the leftover marinade. Heat in a saucepan until thickened. Serve with chicken.

Pumpkin Spice Smoothie

Ingredients:

- 1 cup canned pumpkin puree
- 1 banana
- 1/2 cup Greek yogurt
- 1/2 cup almond milk (or milk of choice)
- 1 tbsp maple syrup
- 1/2 tsp pumpkin pie spice
- 1/4 tsp vanilla extract
- Ice cubes (optional, for thickness)

Instructions:

1. **Blend Ingredients:** In a blender, combine pumpkin puree, banana, Greek yogurt, almond milk, maple syrup, pumpkin pie spice, and vanilla extract. Blend until smooth.
2. **Adjust Consistency:** If desired, add ice cubes and blend again until the smoothie is chilled and thickened.
3. **Serve:** Pour into glasses and enjoy immediately.